Y0-DCF-553

MUSIC MANAGEMENT MADE EASY

PRACTICAL WAYS TO MARKET AND SELL YOUR MUSIC

By Barb Hughes

Hughes/Taylor

Music Management Made Easy

Practical Ways To Market And Sell Your Music

By Barb Hughes

Published by:
Hughes/Taylor
Post Office Box 12550
Portland, Oregon 97212

Library Of Congress Cataloging in Publication Data
Hughes, Barbara L.
Music Management Made Easy: Practical Ways To Market And Sell Your Music/by Barb Hughes.
Illustrated by Barb Hughes
Includes Index
ISBN 1-878036-03-3 12.95 soft cover.

Contents

About the Author

Barb Hughes fell into radio broadcasting in high school. While involved with the Washington State Apple Blossom Festival Royalty she developed an interest in KWWW radio of Wenatchee, Washington. General Manager Jim Corcoran gave her a crack at radio announcing, and she has been infected with the radio bug ever since.

Barb has developed successful radio music programming in medium and major markets and is currently the Music Director for KPDQ's Adult Contemporary program "Upbeat 800" in Portland, Oregon. Barb and her co-worker-husband Chris Taylor do music seminars, write articles for industry trade magazines, are involved in area cable access programs, emcee events, and are in the planning stages of hosting a new video series for teens. They have appeared nationally on the "Live With Regis And Kathie Lee" television program, in *USA Today*, and with Steve Allen in a Christmas radio special. They are volunteer readers for "Open Door", an international Peabody-award-winning radio program. Barb is listed in *Who's Who Of American Women* and a candidate for *Who's Who Of Emerging Leaders In America.*

Barb wrote *Music Management Made Easy* to answer the needs and questions expressed by local and national musicians. Being interested in music and marketing (Barb received two college music scholarships, has two songs copyrighted, and was instrumental in the international marketing success of a Christmas album), Barb wants to help musicians find their niche, develop their marketing plan, and reach their musical goals.

Acknowlegement

Thanks to Jean Gruwell for her fine editing work, and to both Lenore Frimoth and Sheryl Mansfield for their help in computer and printing set-up.

Thanks to the musicians, media, retailers, friends, and other interested people and businesses for their participation and encouragement in this endeavor.

Thanks to Multnomah Press Printing and Graphics department for their fine printing and design work.

Special thanks to my husband Chris and his family for their excitement and support in this project.

WARNING - DISCLAIMER

This book was written to inform and entertain regarding the subject matter covered. The author and publisher are not engaged in giving legal, accounting, or similar professional services. If you need professional or legal assistance, please seek a reputable business in your area.

This book was written as accurately and up-to-date as possible. However, there might be some mistakes in typing and in content. Please use the text as a general guide, not as the only source for your music management research.

The author and Hughes/Taylor shall have neither responsibility nor liability to any person, group, or entity concerning any alleged loss or other damage caused by information directly or indirectly found in this book.

You may return this book to Hughes/Taylor to receive a full refund if you do not wish to be bound by the above statements.

Preface

The purpose of this book is to see your musical goals and aspirations fulfilled. Many musicians have the talent and desire to do something with their music, but are not sure what to "do." This book will help you focus on your goals, and then give you resources to help you attain those goals.

Some musicians have a hard time with the business angle of music. This book will help break down some of those barriers, because it is written in "musician" language, not in "business manager" language. Plus it is written in easy-to-digest segments, with lots of advice, quotes, and humorous anecdotes from music, media, and business professionals.

It is also purposefully written with Portland, Oregon, as the target market, and the Northwest as the secondary market, so that you can see how to apply this information in many useful and practical ways to your area.

Enjoy your journey through *Music Management Made Easy*, and much success in your music!

Barb Hughes

Musician, Who Are You?

This book was written with Portland, Oregon, as the primary market and the Northwest as the secondary market. The principles used in this book can be creatively applied for success in any city and region.

THIS BOOK IS FOR YOU:

1. If you know you love music, but don't know what to do with it.

2. If you are currently performing and want to get more jobs, better advertising, or more money.

3. If you have an album out and want to get local, regional, or national exposure.

4. If you want to make a positive impact in your community, church, or special interest group.

You will also learn: How to target your audience, build a support system, get the jobs you want, get free advertising, how to book your band, how to get radio to play your music, how to get free publicity, how other artists became successful, how to get retail to carry your product, and much more.

The following exercises will help target your special interests, talents, and needs. Your answers will help you best apply your current skill level and music style to get the jobs and opportunities that you desire. Your additional comments will customize this book to become an invaluable tool to aid in your musical and business pursuits.

WHO IS YOUR AUDIENCE?

Exercise #1: Your Music Lifestyle (Which best describes you and your music?)

OUTREACH: The people I know really need help. They like the music I play, and maybe my music and attitude can make a difference in their lives.

VOCATION: I've been into music for as long as I can remember. I sing because I enjoy it, and I can make money at it. Music is my chosen vocation.

WORSHIP: Praise God, I have the opportunity to tell others about Jesus! He has done such a wonderful work in my life, and I want to play music for His glory and honor.

ENJOYMENT: I just like to play! I may not be that good, but I sure have fun!

WHAT ARE YOUR MUSICAL GOALS?

Exercise #2: Your Music Goals   (Which of these best fits you?)

To make money, with music being my chosen vocation
To enjoy the creative art of playing music
To be with friends
To perform
To meet other people with similar goals and talents
To make a positive impact using music
To network
To lead in worship and praise
To have fun
Other

YOUR RECORDING EXPERIENCE

Exercise #3: Your Music Recording Experience (Which best describes you?)

NOVICE: No demo tape. Experience singing/playing at school, church, and service functions. Others seem to enjoy your music and encourage your growth.

AMATUER: Demo tape done on a low budget, not radio quality but great for family, friends, and to get work. Some paying work, and a local following is starting to form which likes your music.

SEMI-PROFESSIONAL: Studio album that is radio quality. Paying work on a consistent basis. Album available for sale to the general public. A loyal following.

PROFESSIONAL: Songs charting nation-wide on radio play lists; national or international distribution of your album. National or international paying concert tours.

YOUR MUSIC SOUND

Exercise #4: Your Music Sound (Choose all that apply)

rock • folk • thrash • rap • inspirational • soft-rock • middle-of-the-road • world music • barbershop • Dixieland • classical • country • sacred • jazz • soul • blue-grass • big-band • ethnic • eclectic • reggae • punk • opera • metal • contemporary "hit" • easy listening • adult-contemporary • noise • urban • hip-hop • black gospel • pop • jazz fusion • instrumental • new age • oldies • R&B • choral • a capella • blues • comedy • other

YOUR PERFORMANCE GOALS

Exercise #5: What Is Your Focus?

What do you want to do with your music?

What is your talent(s) (songwriting, singing, etc.)?

What group (elderly, youth, wealthy, those easily entertained, college age, friends) do you want to perform for?

What do you want to achieve by performing?

Are you currently involved with an ongoing ministry/job that involves the group you want to reach?

What are the results of your work there?

What frustrations do you encounter?

Are you satisfied with the amount of ministry/work you now have? How much time/work do you want?

What methods of advertising and marketing have you used?

Are you willing and able to travel outside Portland (or your immediate area) for jobs?

What equipment and other needs (sound systems, lights, traveling expenses) must be supplied for you to perform?

Would you be comfortable with a set travel fee, a "passing of the hat", and/or the opportunity to sell your albums?

Is there any situation or type of event you would NOT want to play for, such as a wedding, at a bar, a 6th grade camp...?

Is your family supportive of your goals? If not, what compromises would need to be negotiated to make them happy and supportive?

DESCRIPTION OF YOUR MUSIC

To describe your music to others, including prospective employers, the media, friends, and family, fill in the blanks below with your corresponding answers from the previous exercises. You will use your music description throughout the remainder of this book.

I am a(n)_____-oriented musician, a(n)_____
            exercise #1   exercise #3

who performs _____ music. My goal is to_____.
                  exercise #4   exercise #2

"A Musician is a copy artist, an Artist reflects his/her own talents. Both are very important. Some women keep the blues alive by repeating the standard blues numbers and some by writing their own material." (Rhonda Kennedy, *The Clinton Street Quarterly* and KBOO Radio, Portland, OR)

EXAMPLES :

I am a VOCATION-oriented musician, a SEMI-PROFESSIONAL who performs CLASSICAL music. My goal is to MAKE MORE MONEY AND GET MORE JOBS.

I am an OUTREACH-oriented musician, an AMATUER who performs ROCK music. My goal is to ENCOURAGE KIDS.

I am a WORSHIP-oriented musician, a NOVICE who performs INSPIRATIONAL music. My goal is to LEAD IN WORSHIP AND PRAISE.

I am an ENJOYMENT-oriented musician, a NOVICE who performs DIXIELAND music. My goal is to BE WITH FRIENDS.

Who Are You?

"Being a Christian artist is a commitment to *doing* art and not talking about it. In our work, as in our lives, we attempt to maintain that frail balance between the realities of being fallen juxtaposed with the realities of God's grace. The artist works on a 'project', much like a climber works at scaling a mountain. We get to the top and we take in the view. Then it is back down to plan the next climb, knowing that it will be just as difficult as the previous one. Yet, we remember the view." (Jeff Johnson, Ark Records recording artist, Tigard, OR)

Musician—Who Are You?

Your Support Systems

SUPPORT SYSTEMS ARE IMPORTANT!

What happens if you make it big-time and the only people hanging around you are groupies? You need real friends, people who care about you, help you solve problems, and let you know (away from others) when you really did something stupid. People who are honest with you and are THERE for you.

A group of caring people will counsel you against spending big bucks on doing a CD of a rough cut demo tape (a waste of money) even when the CD manufacturer salesman ' assures' you it will sell.

A support group will encourage your family when you are away and emotionally be there when you can not.

A support group will care about you whether your last concert was a flop or a success and can relate to your feelings either way.

A support group knows that you also like to work on cars, read novels, and ride bikes; you don't always have to talk shop with them.

"It's who you know, not where you live. Opportunities are within the parameters of a musician's own talent." (Rick Leachman, Musician and owner of Off Shore Music, Capitola, CA)

WHERE TO FIND SUPPORT GROUPS

To find groups that support your type of music, check the phone book under the headings of Associations, Clubs, Musicians, and Churches. Call your local music store(s) to see if they are aware of any musician organizations in your area. Retail and music stores may also carry local music publications, as well as national music magazines that focus on your style of music, like *Rolling Stone, Sing Out!,* or *CCM.* Recording studios may be aware of support groups or associations both locally and regionally. Colleges are a good source of information.

If your area does not have a support group or club for musicians that meets regularly to exchange ideas, then start one. If your area is small, you may want to put an ad in the paper under the "musical instruments" or "musicians wanted" section. Something simple like:

Musicians' club forming. Call ———— for information.

You may also want to ask local music stores to post your musicians' club information on their bulletin boards, or give your phone number to interested parties. It would be good business for the store to be known as the information center for local musicians, and would most likely increase its business sales as well as enhance its community relations .

"A solid support system within your church is so important - people to keep you accountable outside of the band." (Mylon LeFevre, Starsong recording artist)

If you prefer, you may want to target a specific music style such as:

Classical musicians club forming. Call——— for details.

Metal musicians club forming. Call———for information.

Have your first meeting be informational. Ask what they want out of the club. Examples of musicians' needs could include information on the latest equipment, leads for jobs, ways to make more money, networking, uniting as musicians to support a worthy cause, finding a replacement band member, getting fresh ideas, etc. You will want to discuss dues, if any, and what type of organization you want to be, such as non-profit, a business, a support group, or a club.

You may want to feature guest speakers such as attorneys; music store owners; recording studio, radio, video, or print media experts. Find out the direction the club wants to take, and then meet the needs.

"A Sound Engineer is a performing member of the band, not a static knob-twister. An engineer makes a band sound good and needs to actively participate in the concert, not just tweak a few knobs and go get a coke." (Steve Montague, Northwest Environmental Sound, Portland, OR)

"The best support system a young musician can have is their parents." (Marilynn Peet, Band Manager, Wenatchee, WA)

YOUR SUPPORT SYSTEM: ASSOCIATIONS AND NETWORKS

Examples of Northwest Music Associations and Networks include:

The Portland Music Association   (503)223-9681, P.O. Box 6723, Portland, OR 97228, or 408 S.W. 2nd, Suite 512, Portland, OR 97204.   Current activities include the Mayor's Ball (proceeds go to local charities), a songwriters' contest, and monthly meetings. Future activities anticipated are an awards show and a musicians' referral service.

The Northwest Area Music Association (NAMA)   (206)525-5322, 8315 Lake City Way N.E., Suite 129, Seattle, WA 98115.   Current activities include a yearly music business conference, various classes and seminars of Northwest interest throughout the year, Northwest Area Music Awards, NAMA nights at regional venues, and a newletter.

Christian Musicians' Network   (503)255-0824 or (503)252-2233.   Current activities include various seminars and monthly meetings. Activities in the works are a newsletter, musicians referral service, and monthly prayer meetings.

Jazz Society Of Oregon   (503)234-1332, P.O. Box 968, Portland, OR 97207.   Activities include a newletter, listings of bands, and monthly meetings.

Greater Portland Flute Society   P.O. Box 14521, Portland, OR 97214.

American Federation of Musicians Local 99 (Union) (503) 235-8791, 325 NE 20th, Portland, OR, 97232.

Sweet Adelines (503)239-4323 or (503)282-2906 (national number, 918-622-1444). An educational organization, Sweet Adelines has regional and national quartet and chorus competitions using barbershop harmony. The Vocal Gentry and the Barbership Quartet Society are barbershop organizations for men (national number, 414-654-9111).

In Wenatchee Washington, a loose-knit group of musicians gather for jam sessions at the Orondo Street Pub under the banner of M.U.S.I.C. (Musicians United To Serve In The Community) raising money to provide winter coats and gloves to needy children. By passing the hat during session breaks and at the door, M.U.S.I.C. raises between $300 and $400 per week. They work with the local community action council and the school system to find kids in need, and then individually take each child to a local Sears store (the store helps out with a discount) to help him or her choose a fashionable but practical coat; and M.U.S.I.C. picks up the bill.

MUSICIANS' GROUPS AND COMMUNITY INVOLVEMENT

Your music club/group/association/network may consider entertaining or raising money for a worthy cause or helping out your community in some other tangible way. This is good community relations and keeps your band in the media limelight, which could lead to not only improved public relations but additional work. Some local organizations seeking musician support include :

Union Gospel Ministries. (503)235-3551 All styles of Christian music needed except metal and hard rock for Sunday morning services and men's mission evening services.

Dammasch State Mental Hospital. (503)682-3111 ex 2215. Residents especially appreciate cheery music and instrumentals. (Please no preaching; patients struggle with delusions.)

Doernbecker Childrens Hospital. (503)279-7608. D.C.H. is looking for entertainment for kids aged 4-18. Teens like rock and rap, children enjoy folk, country western, and "kids-type" music. Individuals with guitars are encouraged to travel from room to room. Due to lack of space, large groups are not practical. A piano is available for use. No preaching, please.

YOUR SUPPORT SYSTEM: THE CHURCH

The Church, historically, had some of the best musicians and best artists. It still may, but just does not realize how to support the artists/musicians so that they can excel. How can the church support its musicians? In what creative ways can musicians give back to the church?

"Being understood musically by my wife helps, especially when I drifted into show business. A couple is a team; don't lose sight of that fact. The goal is to win *together*, and one can't be winning when the other feels like s/he is losing. Also, never joke or threaten about getting a divorce. I've seen several entertainment friends split up, and it started as 'just a joke'." (Michael Redman, Musician, Entertainer, and Jingle Singer, Vancouver, WA)

"I've got to have my priorities in order. I serve God first, my family second, and my music comes third. Any time my priorities are not in order I get off-balance." (Melodie Tunney, Jingle Singer and Songwriter, Nashville, TN)

"Nothing keeps my perspective better than to walk off the stage and into a hotel room to change my baby's diaper." (Laural Peters, Musician, Seattle, WA)

WAYS THE CHURCH CAN SUPPORT MUSICIANS

If the church has a newsletter or printing press, use it to promote the musicians' concerts and activites. The bulletin is a great place to start. If you have a church that has regional affiliations, your sister churches may like to be aware of your bands. Allow the musicians access to the press to keep the media and other supporters aware of their concerts and activities.

Do not expect a band to do all things. If a band has a talent and burden for the elderly, allow them the ministry to this group, and support if they want to expand. But they may not be comfortable doing the high school retreat, or the children's ministry.

Pray for your musicians, their families, and their ministries.

Be open to music styles that you have not considered before. The scripture talks of many different music styles, from lamenting to making a joyful noise, from simple, soothing styles to bringing the walls of Jerico down! If God has laid a burden on the hearts of your musical members, discuss their goals, and help focus them in meaningful directions.

Develop a church board of directors to support, guide, and encourage your church musicians.

"When you shoot to be a star, you lose touch with people." (Michael Lewis, Starlight Studios, Tualitin, OR)

When a musician performs for a "free-will" offering, make sure it is actually FREE-will; do not beg, demand, or put a guilt trip on the audience for money. An example of positive wording to collect an offering could be:

"Thank you for being here tonight to hear (musician's) music and ministry. (Musician) really appreciates your support and friendship. At this time, our church would like to give support monetarily to (musician's) ministry because we believe in what he/she is doing. We extend this opportunity to give to (musician's) ministry to everyone."

If the goal of the concert is to raise money for a cause, or music happens to be the vocation of the musician, support the musician in this way also.

WAYS MUSICIANS CAN SUPPORT THE CHURCH

Accept the counsel of your church. Ask questions. Express your goals and concerns. Find out what needs are unmet musically within your church and help to fill the voids you are capable of. Some examples include:

Does your church support a home for un-wed mothers? Work together with the womens Sunday school group. The women can knit booties or collect baby clothes. You can prepare your band with music that is stylistically what the mothers would enjoy. The band and the womens group then make an appointment to perform at the un-wed mothers home, the band puts on a great concert, and the women pass out "goodies" to the mothers and mothers-to-be.

Does your church support missionaries in Africa? England? Russia? Have the Sunday school group write letters to missionaries to find out what spiritual struggles they and their people are having. Then have the class write poetry and prose, using scripture and their own words, to encourage the missionaries. Your band can write a song and the class can help sing it on a tape, along with reading their prose and encouragements. Mail the tape (and a recorder if needed) to the missionary.

Lead a Sunday school or class in the study of hymns of the church, or of contemporary Christian music. Find out who wrote the songs and why. Learn some of the songs, and then take the class "caroling" to rest homes. Even little children can become involved with this type of ministry. If they learn a song such as "Angels Watching Over Me" they can make a soft art project glueing eyes, felt feet, and paper wings onto a yarn-type ball, and give these "little angels" to rest home residents. The kids learn a song that will encourage them, they learn how to give to others, and they spread a lot of God's love in the meantime!

Help out in other ways, too, if you can. Help wash dishes at the youth reteat, if youth is your ministry focus. You will learn a lot more about where the youth are coming from if you are right in the middle of their day-to-day activities. Plus they see you as more accessible, and you can develop the type of friendship that has an effect over and above your musical influence.

Join the church choir. Get involved by performing music during Church services and special occasions.

If your church does not have a music program, start one that meets the needs of the current congregation. If they are mostly 75-year-old women, the program will most likely be more hymn or folk-oriented. If the current congregation is mostly young families, find out their favorite styles of music and present the message in that way.

If you are currently a worship leader, take on an interested 'disciple' or two and teach them how to lead in worship. It will be good for the church to have a back up when you go on vacation, or if you decide to expand into another area.

"CHRISTIAN" MUSIC

No style of music is more "Christian" than any other style. In fact, many of the eighteenth century hymns were written to familiar bar tunes so that the common people could sing along!

To help clarify "Christian" music, you need to decide if you are writing and singing **Christian Principled** music or **Christian Targeted** music.

Christian Principled music might be about love, nature, daily problems, and personal feelings written from a Christian point of view, and targeted towards a mainsteam audience.

Christian Targeted music might cover such subjects as forgiveness, Heaven, and the person and work of Jesus Christ.

Christian Targeted music is directed towards those who are Christian, and is meant for encouragement, teaching, outreach, and food-for-thought with the Christian community in mind. Music can be **Christian Principled** and targeted towards the Christian community; however, if music is **Christian Targeted,** some mainstream audiences are lost due to lack of understanding of traditional church words and phrases.

CHURCH LEADERS' COMMENTS TO LOCAL MUSICIANS

"God has given to musicians their families as their first priority. If you trash your family in the name of ministry, then it's NOT God's will. You need a source of accountability and support, a group who holds you accountable for who you are musically and how God wants to use you. Music has that powerful ability to communicate, and we need theological integrity in the music we perform within the church. A lot of Christmas information our society holds has been gained through Christmas carols, and many of those are theologically incorrect. We need to make music that speaks truth." (Drew Hulse, Columbia Presbyterian Church, Vancouver, WA)

"When you travel to other churches to perform, write down the names of the pastor, his wife and family, and other greeter people you come in contact with. Write down a little bit about each one. Also note what you are wearing and what songs you perform. This way, the next time you are in town to do a concert, you can make the pastor and others feel comfortable by 'remembering' them. Plus you won't end up playing the same songs and wearing the same clothes that you did the previous concert at the same church." (Mary McGinnis, *Church Guide*, Portland, OR)

"In our church we see music as a ministry first, entertainment second. If a band's soul desire is to play rock-n-roll music, without any thought towards using that music to praise God, then it doesn't belong in our church service. I feel that music is very important to all ages, especially to young people as an outreach tool. Eightyfive percent of people in our culture who have made commitments to Jesus have done so by the age of nineteen, ninetyfive percent before the age of twentyone. As a youth pastor, I feel the urgency to reach young people in a language they understand, with a message to change their lives in a positive way." (Rob Neushwander, Glad Tidings Church, Vancouver, WA)

"Christians who are musicians need to figure out up front what their ministry focus is. Are you interested in evangelism, worship, reconciliation of the family, Christian entertainment, mainstream entertainment as a Christian performer, or what? All are equally valid, but you do need to make a choice. If your band has not found their focus, they may potentially offend the church by playing in a bar, or confuse a non-believer who saw the band in a bar, by playing on a church stage. None of the options are wrong or bad, just do not confuse them. Discern God's purpose for your ministry. If you are an evangelist, what are you doing in churches all the time? Focus is equally important for me as an administrater to think and pray about the spiritual goals of each concert before I book a band. I want first of all to see an artist's heart before I book him/her. I ask him/her, 'How's your marriage?' or 'When's the last time you had personal time in the Word?.' If the artists are willing to be transparent and honest, then I'm willing to work with him/her. You don't have to be perfect, just forgiven, as the saying goes." (Deborah Greenidge, New Hope Community Church, Portland, OR)

"Talk to your pastor and find out if your denomination has a general or district assembly that could use your musical talents. If you perform at an assembly, chances are you will get several requests from those who attended to sing at their individual home churches." (Royce Mitchell, Portland First Nazarene Church, Portland, OR)

"Encourage your Christian musicians to meet for fellowship, and to perform their songs for one another. In this way, they will build confidence, maturity, and practical performing skills." (Steve Carlson, Calvary Chapel. Portland, OR)

YOUR SUPPORT SYSTEM: THE FAMILY

Your "family" may consist of mom, dad, siblings, grandparents, aunts, uncles, and countless cousins. Your "family" may consist of your spouse and the cat. Your "family" may be very close college friends. Whatever your definition of family, they are an important support system for you. You will be baring your soul and talent to the general public, and you need a safe, warm, accepting place to relax and rejuvinate.

HOW THE FAMILY CAN SUPPORT THE MUSICIAN

Talk about the musician's band to your friends and associates when appropriate. Others may know of available work, networks, and associations. It also makes the musician feel that you are proud of him/her and their work.

When the musician gets home from a concert, share his/her enthusiasm or listen to his/her laments.

If you can, go to the concerts that your musician invites you to. It really helps him/her to know that you are in the audience.

Make a healthy lunch or snack for the musician before he/she leaves on a short trip.

Ask if you can help pack anything.

Remember that musicians are doing a job when they perform, even though it looks as if they are just out having fun. They have a lot on their minds (will the sound system work? Will the audience be responsive? Did I bring Certs?...) Be patient; they will be easier to talk to after the concert.

Be aware that musicians have a sensitivity to feeling real or perceived acceptance or rejection. Musicians tend to be intense and need you to share and accept them in an understanding way.

Get involved in the musician's passion. If you are strong, help in set up and tear down. If you have good phone presence, offer to do booking or confirm concerts/club dates. People support that which they help to create, and if you take an active roll in your musician's work, you will naturally become more interested, involved, and supportive of it. Plus you will discover new talents and challanges, and have fun in the process!

HOW THE MUSICIAN CAN SUPPORT THE FAMILY

Invite your spouse (or family) with you to events, and introduce them. This way the fans see that you have a respect for and commitment to your spouse, and you get less flirtation. Your spouse will feel more secure, also. Sometimes it is scary to see your artistic spouse swarmed by good-looking people of the opposite sex. You need to show your spouse that you love, are commited to, and proud of him/her.

Include spouses in the group fun and activities before the concert.

If you travel to another city to do a concert, bring back a gift for your spouse and family.

One of your biggest obstacles is that your spouse thinks you are just out having fun, and you think that your spouse is just relaxing at home. Remember that you both are doing a job that is important.

If you know you will be going away for a weekend, try to work it out so that you can take off the Friday before or the Monday after to be with your family.

Call home regularly when you are on the road.

If your family travels with you, make sure that they have appropriate accommodations.

Make sure that your family has money when you are gone, that the kitchen is well stocked, and that the car has gas.

Avoid being gone over five nights in a row if possible.

"Music is a part of a person's being. What I play is part of me." (Don Bankhead, Locals Only, Portland, OR)

"I take the 30/70 approach for success - expect that you'll succeed about 30% of the time. You can make a tremendous impact with a 30% success rate; just take a look at baseball players! If you know going in that there are rough times then you can deal with the failure. Ask God to guide you, and if He has something better for you, then go for it. If you're failing 100% of the time, then it is time to seek another road. Sometimes you just need to turn the music off for a season." (Michael Redman, Musician, Entertainer, and Jingle Singer, Vancouver, WA)

"Don't go into teaching unless you want to teach. Teaching music involves a lot of extracurricular time; you're with the band during basketball and football games, there are evening choir and band concerts, in addition to the daily classes. Teaching music has to be fun for *you* if you want to instill a love of music to kids. If you have the attitude of, 'I can't get a job performing, so I guess I'll teach,' you will do more harm to your class then good." (Dr Stan Sanford, Portland State University, Portland, OR)

SCHOOLS AND COLLEGES

Schools and colleges are aware of music societies, such as the American Choral Directors' Association, Music Educators' National Conference, and the (Oregon) Music Teachers' Association (each state has its own branch), and students often receive reduced rates on membership fees.

Bulletin boards may be available listing musicians, instruments for sale, or music networking opportunities. Some colleges have referral services for student musicians who want wedding, funeral, or reception music experience. Most college music programs have resources available.

Call the college music departments and ask if they have a faculty member who plays your particular instrument. Inquire about support systems, networking, and other opportunities.

For nine years Portland State University has participated in a program called "Clarinet Day" where grade school through high school clarinet students are invited to a one day workshop, ending with a recital. About 20 area music teachers and faculty donate their time.

"If you pursue a career as an artist, then be yourself. If you are a hired musician, be who your employer wants you to be. If you are a studio musician, then you need the proper equipment to do the job right. It is important to get to know people professionally by your hard work and not by being a fanatic." (Blair Masters, Keyboardist and Session Player, Nashville, TN)

"Know who you can trust, and maintain creative balance." (Teri Reed, Northwest Area Musicians Association, Seattle, WA)

WORKSHEET

1. What support systems are available in your area?

2. Which support systems are you currently involved with?

3. Which additional support systems would help you reach your goals?

Marketing and Publicity

Know Your Market : These three words form the basis of reaching your goals. The saying, "If you aim for nothing, that's what you get," is invariably true in music marketing also.

MARKETING TO RADIO

Only send your tapes to the industry people who specialize or generalize in your style of music. This will take some investigating on your part, but will be worth it in time, money, and your mental health. Why set yourself up for needless rejection?

Example: If you play country music, do not send your tapes to classical radio stations; your tapes will go straight into the garbage. That would be a waste of your money and the classical music director's time.

If your local country station agrees to play your tape, ask for a letter of recommendation that you can send to regional country stations. The radio sales department probably has books that list names, addresses, phone numbers, and other important information. One such publication is *Spot Rate And Data.* Your local library may also have a resource book of national radio stations.

Subscribe to a national publication specializing in your music style to see what radio stations in your region are industry leaders, and send your tape to those, along with a cover letter and local recommendation.

Sometimes there may be a "market within the market". Your favorite rock station may only play classic rock, and therefore not play any new product. Your favorite Christian station may only play pop or middle-of-the-road music, and therefore not play any country, rock, or rap.

If you play something eclectic like Bavarian whale music, do not plan on the mainstream market welcoming your music with open arms. However, new age and alternative stations may appreciate this type of musical innovation.

If you are a musician who plays primarily traditional Irish, Spanish, African, or other ethnic music, then market primarily towards ethnic programs, publications, and markets to form your base audience.

Example: You might take advantage of holidays to promote your music to the mainstream audience, or to broaden your market. A pop, rock, or "Zoo-type" radio station may play a well-produced Irish song on St. Patrick's Day; an Italian-laced love song might be played near Valentine's Day.

MARKETING TO PRINT MEDIA

Find out what local publications are open to print local concert, club, and benefit information. Sources aware of local music- scene publications include music stores, recording studios, radio stations, local printing companies, the local newpaper (they are usually aware of any "competition"), and library resources such as *Gayle Directory Of Publications*. Get a copy of each local

publication so you know what audience/music it is aimed at. See how the articles are written, and if there is a charge to have your concert/music information included. Many times the papers will print your information for free, and some local newspapers have an Arts & Entertainment section. Your music is "news" that they can sell.

Researching the publication criteria for inclusion is important. Why try to get your metal band listed in *Opera Digest?* The markets just do not match.

When researching publications to send your information to, notice how other write-ups have been worded, and do accordingly. If the norm is only to include name, number, and music style, include that information. If it includes the above plus ticket price, size of venue, and a bio (biography) of your band, send everything that they will use.

MARKETING TO TELEVISION AND VIDEO

If you have a visually stimulating presentation, you may consider television, cable access, or other forms of video. A good place to start looking for leads is the yellow pages under public broadcasting, television, cable systems, and even colleges. Call these places and ask if they have any TV or cable programming that features local musicians. If they do, ask about their criteria for inclusion. If you or your band fit the criteria, you may be on your way to television or cable experience, and possibly a free video of your band. (see media chapter for details)

MARKETING HONESTLY

Be true to your goal and your sound. If your music is folk, do not claim to be the next Prince or Madonna. For ease of introduction, it may be helpful for you to describe your music style by naming an artist in your field whose style is similar to yours. You do not always have to do this, but for initial introduction it helps pique the interest of your prospective client.

As a music director, the author is aware of times where slick packaging was matched with an inconsistent recording.... a CD where a five second count ended in hearing a cassette click on, followed by singers and all instrumentation recorded at one mike.

Dress and present yourself in a way that conveys your music style and music experience level. If you have a dynamic sound, make sure your album packaging and bio are top notch also. It is better to do it right than to spend almost enough and have a product that does not sell.

"One of the best ways to get jobs is to have a good presentation to give to club owners. A promotional package that includes a demo tape, bio on all band members, a picture, and articles from media sources would be excellent. In order to get jobs, develop a local following and a mailing list of this following to mail out band info and updates. This way your fans can come hear you, the club owner makes money, and you'll be hired again." (Bonnie Carter, *Positively Entertainment*, Portland, OR)

MARKETING YOUR DEMO TAPE

If you have a demo recording, do not expect commercial radio stations to play it. However, DO make it available at concerts and clubs for a nominal fee. (How could a three song demo cassette of an unknown artist sell for $10 when a full album of a favorite national group sells for $8.95?) DO use your demo to get jobs. DO use your demo as a rough idea to present to a professional recording facility if/when you want to do an album for radio play. DO use your demo for Christmas gift giving and personal music enjoyment.

Many times famous musicians have been influenced by lesser known folk, gospel, or jazz artists. Your talent may not be performing for the mainstream public but to inspire *other* musicians.

PUBLICITY

There are a lot of local resources for free advertising of entertainment and social activities. When they print your concert information, other people will buy their publication to find out what is going on. You are actually "news" that sells papers for them, so take advantage of the joint opportunity to help each other out.

"To get performances, it takes a lot of hard work, hours on the phone, and the ability to 'toot your own horn'." (Deanna Callaway, Sweet Adelines, Portland, OR)

SEND CONCERT INFORMATION TO:

Local radio stations and newpapers that apply to your music.

High schools and colleges if your music is targeted towards youth. Address information to "Student Body Officers." That will make them feel important, plus they have a hand in organizing many school events that involve music.

Clubs and lodges if your music is aimed at parties and banquets.

Associations interested in your style of music or focus. "Associations" in the phone book covers such diverse groups as "Oregon Funeral Directors Association" and "National Association Of Pastoral Musicians."

When you send the media information about your concert, if it is an event that costs money, send a few tickets and a personal invitation to all radio, newpaper, associations, and agencies that you contact. This personal touch could gain you invaluable contacts, plus get key people to see you in concert.

Local retail stores that are currently carrying your music or those you would like to carry your music in the future. If they see that you are regularly performing, they will be more inclined to carry and stock your product. This also helps in name familiarity, possible job leads, and encourages interaction between artist and retail.

Write your musical opinions and editorials to local music publications and newspaper editors, as well as to appropriate trade magazines and newsletters.

If your articles get printed, use a copy or quote from the article in your portfolio.

Call public, religious, and college radio stations and find out what programs are locally produced. Contact these sponsors and ask if they would consider having local artists sing or perform music on their shows. Even if your original music can not be used, maybe you can write a theme song or help out with effects.

The chamber of commerce may be a resource for conventions.

One of the best ways to get media attention is a feature story or news article about something community-oriented that your band is involved in. If you are helping others with your music, alert the media! A feature article has more impact than an advertisement for an album, and many times the exposure is free.

"Portland is viewed as a musician's Camelot. Musicians can get their concert information printed for free in several local papers, work is fairly easy to find, and musicians get paid for their work. In the Bay area, musicians have a waiting list to get into clubs, and have to pay for just about everything. The Portland music scene is very exciting and productive in the industry." (Rhonda Kennedy, *Clinton Street Quarterly*, and KBOO Radio, Portland, OR)

HOW TO START YOUR OWN RADIO SHOW

If you have radio and video programs that air local talent in your area, do not re-invent the wheel. Take advantage of the programs that are already in progress.

If you live in a small town, and there are no radio stations that play local music, maybe it is because they do not have the budget to hire someone to start such a program. Or it could be that they do not realize how much quality local/regional music is available. Volunteer your time to head up a project to look into local/regional music as a viable alternative for your local radio station. Organize other local musicians and network with those in your state and region to get enough product to warrant a show, and you may be able to convince a local radio station to let you program a half-hour of music a week.

Talk to local music stores, recording studios, and other local musicians to see if they would be interested in monetarily sponsoring such a program. (This is where a musicians' association would come in handy.)

You would be basically buying a block of radio air time, so you would talk to the sales manager or an account executive. The music you select may need to fit into the already established programming format, or you may be able to buy a time slot on a weekend or all-night, and get the opportunity to play whatever you want, since you paid for the time. Discuss your options with the radio sales representative.

Money talks in the radio business, too, and the advertising benefits for the sponsors of a well-done program would be great. The sponsors would be seen as the movers and shakers of the local music scene, and good local music would be heard on the radio.

COMMUNITY ATTITUDE

The attitude of your town plays a large part in your success. Small communities may be more comfortable with soft rock or country music. If your goal is to make money with your music, find out what is popular in your community and cater to that musical taste.

If your music is not accepted by the general public, you may be able to target a certain group. Junior high kids might be an audience for positive-message rap artists. If your goal is to express your art, college audiences are usually fairly open to different music styles.

If you are planning a concert in another town, send a bio, concert itinerary, and tape, if possible, to appropriate local interest groups, radio, and print media. The free publicity will make the town more aware of you and your music, and you will have a more enthusiastic, larger crowd in attendance.

Not all media sources will publish your information for free. If they are advertisement-only publications or radio stations, do not nag them to give you free advertising. Be grateful for the freebies, and pay for what you deem necessary.

THE BAND BIO

Think of a bio as a sales tool. When you are looking for music work, unless you know the person hiring you or get lucky, you may need some sort of informational package to "sell" yourself and your music to prospective employers.

A bio is very helpful for the musician. You may want a one page description of who you are and a black-and-white photo.

You may want to use a notebook or folder to hold articles, pictures, and other information.

A resume' may fit the bill also, or a combination of the above.

Possible things to include would be: band name, address and phone number, band picture(s), music style(s) performed, articles and critiques, a list of radio stations playing your material, a list of albums out and where they can be purchased, and any other interesting tidbits that make your band stand out in the crowd.

Another option is to hire a publicist, agency, or marketing service. Check the phone book or ask other musicians for referrals. Find out what the agency criteria are, and see if what you need matches up with what they can provide.

Sue Brent is a publicist for semi-professional bands who already have albums and now need recording contracts. Sue's main interest is in rock and pop music and has represented such local bands as Nero's Rome, Rex and the Rockits, and Caryl Mack. Sue's contacts nationally with *Billboard* and *Musician*, as well as her awareness of local happenings, keep her in the forefront of Portland's music scene. Her criteria for bands are:

Semi-professional band or individual
Radio quality album available for sale to the public
Rock or pop music styles
Good attitude
Group or individual ready to go national

"The key to success is promotion and cooperation."
(Craig Mayther, President, Portland Music Association, Portland, OR)

You may want to check out management agencies, such as Nathan Sakany Creative Management Agency in Lynnwood, WA. Services include management development, booking, public relations, publicity, photography, and more.

BAND "GOODIES"

If you do weddings, clubs, and such, have business cards so that your clients can do repeat business with you, or pass your card on to other interested parties.

Depending on your audience and budget, other paraphernalia may profit you and your customers:

Rock and country fans like to buy posters and wear T-shirts that show the band name, logo, or picture.

Classical and jazz audiences might go for a classy pen with your name and number.

You might use a small gift as part of your marketing. If you do weddings, consider giving the couple an autographed picture of the band.

Stickers with your band name, picture, or logo would be nifty give-aways at grade school and junior high gatherings.

"When a band has something worthwhile to say, then they become popular." (Fiona Martin, *Willamette Week*, Portland, OR)

**Are you <u>sure</u> you can't play this?
Side Two has synthesized harpsichord. . .**

WORKSHEET

1. Create a band bio or update your current bio.

2. Get business cards.

3. See *Finding And Booking Work* chapter for how to cold call, and for further information on getting jobs.

4. See *Media* chapter for radio, publication, television and other media information.

Finding and Booking Work

Where do you find jobs and how do you book them? The phone book is a wonderful tool. Depending on your music style and venue preferences, you will have quite a variety of prospects to choose from. Look in the phone book under: clubs, organizations, entertainers, music, theatre, wedding, funeral, youth organizations, associations, churches, agencies, hospitals, colleges and schools, restaurants, banquet rooms, etc.

The businesses and jobs that want your type of music will be happy you called. Clubs need music; churches have functions that need music; most associations have parties at Christmas, New Years, and more. You *do* have a market. Be honest with your skill level, and do not be embarrased to call.

PHONE TECHNIQUE: WHAT TO SAY

What do you say on the phone when you "cold-call?" It depends what type of organization you are calling, but the general idea is the same. The following examples may help you find your own wording for cold-calling.

"Play for as many people as you can whether it be 5 or 500. You need to be seen to get that local following." (Renee Garcia, Reunion recording artist)

Phone Technique Examples To Obtain Jobs:

(club)   "Hi, could I please speak to the person who books bands for the (name of club)? Thank you." "Hi, I'm (name) with the band (band's name) and we play (style of music). We would like to play at your club. What criteria do you use to select bands?" (Do they audition before they hire, do they book only a certain style of music, do they want copy bands or original music, do they need a bio and tape before they consider a musician?) "Thank you for your time and this information. I'll get the information to you tomorrow."

(wedding service agency) "Hello, could I please speak to the person who arranges music for your wedding service? Thank you." "Hello, my name is (name) and I sing (style of music). Could I send a tape of my work for you to review with the possibility of freelancing my music with your wedding service company?" "What other information would you like me to send?" "Thank you for you time. I'll get that information to you tomorrow."

Phone Technique Examples To Talk To Media:

Knowing exactly what you want gets results. When the author called the Portland area radio stations to find who plays local and regional music, the conversation went something like this:

(station)   "Hello, KZZZ radio, Patti speaking."

(author)   "Hi Patti, I'd like to know if KZZZ is open to playing local or regional music."

(station)   "That's a good question. Let me connect you with the Music Director." (pause) "Hi, Joe Smith. What can I do for you?"

(author)   "Hello Mr. Smith. I'd like to know if KZZZ is open to playing local or regional music."

(station)   "It depends...."

(author)   "What are your criteria for airplay?"

(station)   "Well, they have to be on CD or good vinyl, fit into our regular format, have product available in stores, and be performing regularly."

(author)   "Thank you Mr. Smith, that's what I needed to know."

Do not beat around the bush with the receptionist or try to get past her to "someone important." If you do this, you will probably end up on hold, or not able to get the information that you need.

In most businesses, the person answering the phone is your direct link to the information that you need. Respect that person.

"Don't hand-write your cover letter. Your promotional material and demo are your first impression, and if it's not professional, clients will be less inclined to accept your music no matter how valid it is. Rent a typewriter if necessary." (Kim Char Meredith, Island Awaken Music, Honolulu, HI)

You might consider using a talent agency. An agent will do most of your booking, and leave you free to concentrate exclusively on your music.

Look in the phone book or ask around for referrals. Ask your current customers for referrals.

Have business cards available to give out at your performances and concerts.

Local musician Bill Price has a detailed booking, publicity, and marketing campaign. With a combination of file folders, phone calling, letters, and personal contact, Bill manages to keep his business running smoothly. Bill also utilizes a radio promotions organization, has direct support from his church (Rolling Hills Community), and his family.

"Many times smaller communities are more excited to see a concert than larger cities. Why should big cities be excited over an 'unknown' artist when they can see national entertainment on a regular basis? On a free-will offering I made $26 at a big city concert, and turned right around and made $500 at a small town concert." (Mary McGinnis, Musician, Portland, OR)

"Big hotels book New Year's music sometimes a year in advance. If they are happy with what you do, they will most likely book you again for the next year. December seems to be one of the busiest months for musicians, with business Christmas parties, New Year's parties, and increased seasonal music work. There are always weddings to do and clubs to play. Make sure you have a bio ready to present for work, be prepared to audition, and keep bugging them!" (Rick Leachman, Musician and owner of Off Shore Music, Capitola, CA)

CLUBS

Traditional clubs can be found in the phone book, by word-of-mouth, and in local music newspapers. Alternative clubs are sometimes harder to find and are springing up all over the country. Some in the Portland area include:

The Connection (503)775-1806. An alcohol-free, smoke-free club featuring Northwest Christian pop, rock, and R&B bands, with plans in the future to expand into jazz, inspirational, and others.

Cafe Mocha (503)288-9950. Alcohol-free club featuring just about every style of music from new-age to ethnic, from country to folk.

Club Revelation (206)694-2063. Alcohol-free, smoke-free club for teenagers. Includes live music, pool tables, open gym, video games and more.

Sunnyside Coffee House (503)235-6362. Catering to street people and the homeless, services and activities include free food, live music, movies, and an open gym.

"I have friends who make phone calls for a living, and they have volunteered to do my booking on their breaks." (Royce Mitchell, Musician, Portland, OR)

One of the best ways to get started making money in music is to learn top 40, classic rock, and pop songs. These will be the most requested club, dance, and reception tunes.

Make sure you know what the going rate is for bands in your area, and be prepared to quote a price. Some clubs give you a percentage of the evening's profits. Some pay a flat fee plus tips. Find out beforehand so you know what to expect.

Cover bands make good, consistent income by playing other artists' music. The catch is, there is limited creativity and limited possibilities for national exposure. Original bands may not make much income to begin with but have a greater earning potential due to the possibilities for national exposure of their creativity.

There is a distinctive difference between the music industry and the entertainment industry. The **music industry** caters to creativity of artists and the developing of a signature style(s). Artists are allowed to enjoy the passion of making their own unique music and encouraged to live, dream, and breathe it. The music industry artist's supreme goal is to create beauty.

The **entertainment industry** is looking for employees to provide energy and entertainment that will excite their particular clientele. They want employees to perform mostly cover material made famous by other bands. The club or entertainment owner has built up a reputation and is looking for employees willing and able to add value to their establishment.

It is important to take advantage of local performing opportunities. Contact music stores, recording studios, and music networking organizations for information concerning showcases. The BMI Showcase, The Mayor's Ball, and The Byte are Portland area showcases for local and Northwest talent that will lend credibility to your music.

A professional bio package, song list, and a band's maturity level are also important. Different clubs hire different styles of music. Find clubs that appreciate your sound, and play there. If there are fifteen clubs in town and only one caters to an audience which appreciates your style of music, then play at the one club and give that audience your very best.

The *wrong* reasons to be in the music or entertainment industry include: To pick up "chicks", to be a part of a big party scene, to trash the club's furniture, to make big bucks, to make an easy living, or to become popular.

Playing clubs is work. The club is not hiring you to get drunk, they are hiring you to play familiar music that their clientele will like and can dance to, and that will increase the clubs profitability margin. Clubs that want your original music will let you know, otherwise be prepared to play cover music. Either way, perform the music that you were hired to do. If you try to slip your own adgenda past the club owner, you probably will not be hired back and may even be blackballed in your club community.

- -

"If motivation for a musician is stardom, then he/she may spend their entire life seeking it, and may never find it. Being a "star" isn't necessarily what it's cracked up to be." (Deni Herrmann, Pacific Talent Inc., Portland, OR)

CONTRACTS

Always have everything in writing. It makes both parties feel more comfortable if they know what to expect and what is expected of them. Even people with the best intentions can forget a detail or two (like how much they promised to pay), so make sure it is in writing and both artist and employer have a copy and agree to all terms.

Make sure the customer, not the musician, is responsible for insuring the event.

Most bands have contract forms they have found successful for their particular needs. Ask your band friends for a sample copy of their contract, talk to a recording studio for ideas or, better yet, consult your attorney. Attorneys have legal forms for everything, and you could save yourself a lot of headaches by having a solid contract in the first place.

CREATIVE ALTERNATIVES FOR MUSIC TALENT

If your goal as a band is to make money, but your band concert income is not enough to live off yet, consider supplementing the music you love with alternative music work.

"Videos are a very powerful way of communicating your songs. If you can swing it, get some type of video together. It's good promotional material and it lends credibility to your group." (Kyle Justice, Eyrie Film & Video, Vancouver, WA)

Seminars: If you like kids, do seminars at high schools, colleges, and youth retreats on instrument technique, music history, or any other musical area of interest to you and your target audience. For publicity, post a band picture with the activity information on a bulletin board where kids congregate. Put all the essentials on the poster such as time, place, cost, etc.

Teaching and lessons: Private music lessons are an option. Contact music stores for advice on how to start up, or if they are looking to hire teachers in your particular field. You can also teach from your home, from the student's home, or in a classroom situation.

Endorsements: If you have a loyal local following, consider approaching a compatible store, studio, or other merchandiser, to endorse their products. You get media exposure by being seen in their advertisements, and they get a local "celebrity" to endorse their product free, or for a reasonable fee.

Studio work: Check local recording studios to see if they have need of musicians with your experience, ability, and instrument for future album projects.

Voice talent/acting: Register yourself with a talent agency. Consider ad work using both voice talent and acting.

"Musicians need to build a following by singing anywhere. Sing at church, ask your friends if you can sing at their church, sing the national anthem at Beaver Baseball games, Blazer Basketball games, and school graduations. Request the PA announcer to announce where your tapes are available, if possible." (Carl Parker, Musician, Portland, OR)

Copywriting: If you are a good lyricist, you may be a candidate for copywriting. Consider copywriting for small radio stations or advertising companies on a consignment or per piece produced basis.

Sales/secretarial: If you like just being around music, consider music store sales, reception/secretarial work at a recording studio, or record store sales. You will be able to see a different side of the industry, keep up on trends, and get inside information.

Media volunteering: Public radio and cable access are great places to get hands-on experience in the music-media field. Be willing to do anything to get in...sweep floors, take the required classes, etc. Your enthusiastic attitude, ability to learn, and willingness to do even the most menial tasks will move you quickly to areas of interest.

Engineering: Take classes or learn hands-on from a friend who already engineers for bands. Bands are always looking for good light and sound engineers, and you could probably carve out fairly consistent work if you are good.

Music Therapy: Willamette University in Salem, Oregon, offers degrees in music therapy. Portland Adventist Hospital uses music therapy in their psychiatric units, with stroke patients, and for eating disorders. Music is also used to control pain, aid in relaxation, and boost the immune system. Even for relatively healthy people music can be used as a pick-me-up or for relaxation. Use your music to heal your community.

Find out what creative ways you can use your particular music style to become involved in your community. When people see and hear you performing, they are more likely to hire you.

**Take 10 minutes of pop now,
10 minutes of easy listening tonight,
and call me tomorrow.**

WORKSHEET

1. What type of work do you want?

2. List organizations that could supply the type of work you desire.

3. Create a cold-calling technique that applies to your personality and goals.

4. List local and regional talent agencies.

5. Create or update your business contract form.

The Media

LOCAL PRINT MEDIA

To find local and regional publications interested in listing your band or doing a feature article on you, check out music stores, neighborhood associations, the phone book, recording studios, radio stations, and the library. The following are examples of Northwest publications interested in the local and regional music scene.

Willamette Week (503)243-2122. Weekly publication of news and entertainment.

This Week Magazine (503)682-1223. Local interest paper delivered to every doorstep weekly.

ACM Journal P.O. Box 1273 Sumner, WA 98390. Monthly publication of alternative, religious, political, and college art and music.

happening! (206)546-7350. Monthly northwest guide to christian concerts and entertainment.

"Success is reflecting the inner truth. If a musician is true to his/her calling, then they are a success." (Rhonda Kennedy, KBOO and *The Clinton Street Quarterly*, Portland, OR)

LOCAL NEWSPAPERS

The following examples of regional and colleg
newspapers and national music publications wer
gleaned from the library reference book *Gale Directoi
Of Publications.*

Newspaper Feature Editors, Oregon:

Portland: *The Oregonian* 1320 SW Broadway Portlanc
OR 97201. Music: Stu Tomlinson (503)221-8223

Eugene: *The Register Guard* P.O. Box 10188 Eugene
OR 97440-2188. Music: Jim Godbold (503)485-1234.

Salem: *Statesman Journal* 280 Church St NE Salem, OF
97301.
Music: Ron Cowan (503)399-6728

Newspaper Feature Editors, Washington:

Seattle: *Seattle Post-Intelligencer* 101 Elliot Ave W Seattle
WA 98119. Music: Richard Campbell (206)448-8396

Seattle: *Times* P.O. Box 70 Seattle, WA 98111. Music:
Melinda Bargreen (206)464-2321

Spokane: *The Spokesman Review* P.O. Box 2160 Spokane,
WA 99210. Music: Dan Webster (509)459-5493

Tacoma: *The Morning News Tribune* P.O. Box 11000
Tacoma, WA 98411. Music: Patrick McCoid (206)597-
8675

Everett: *The Herald* P.O. Box 930 Everett, WA 98206.
Music: Linda Bryant (206)339-3430

xamples Of College Newpapers:

he Siskiyou: Southern Oregon State College, Ashland,)R.

roadside: Central Oregon Community College, Bend,)R.

he Barometer: Oregon State University, Corvallis, OR.

)ld Oregon: University Of Oregon, Eugene, OR.

he Torch: Lane Community College, Eugene, OR.

)acific Index: Pacific University, Forest Grove, OR.

:astern Beacon: Eastern Oregon State College, La ;rande, OR.

:he Mountain Guide: Blue Mountain Community :ollege, Pendleton, OR.

The Beacon: University Of Portland, Portland, OR.

The Bridge: Portland Community College, Portland, OR.

)ioneer Log: Lewis And Clark College, Portland, OR.

:ourier 4: Chemeketa Community College, Salem, OR.

The Cresent: George Fox College, Newberg, OR

"Do your research. Have a plan and an example of your product (i.e. video or album). You usually can't sell an idea; there has to be effort put into a product, with the product available to others." (Frank Harlan, Bombshelter Videos, Seattle, WA)

CABLE ACCESS AND TELEVISION

Call Cable Access and Television stations (found in the phone book) and ask if they are open to playing local and regional music videos. If they are aware of any, they will connect you with local and regional shows/producers of programs that spotlight local activity. Northwest television and cable access programs that are looking for talent include the following:

Rose City TV Production/TCI Cable Vision Of Oregon (503)243-7458. Cable access channel 33 community facilitator, Mary Avalon, will provide all the equipment and experience you need to make your own video FREE. All that you need to provide is the time and the talent.

The Video Access Project   (503)295-6655. Producer Rosemary Jane is looking for any type of music and entertainment (except religious). Her crew will film you FREE, and the public is welcome to watch the filming.

KPDX TV 49/ The Other Guy Presents Northwest Music (503)239-4949. Co-producers Bobby Castaneda (cast-ah-neet-ah) and Dale Turnbull will produce your video or tape you live. Any style of music is acceptable for this half-hour weekly program, and it is FREE to you.

"The key to getting a good video of a band is for the producer to listen to and get to know the band to be filmed. This way the character of the band can shine through, and we get a better video tape." (Gustavia Miller, Paragon Cable, Portland, OR)

Multnomah Cable Access/Paragon Cable (503)667-7636. Rose Read, Community Program Coordinator, will direct you to FREE classes on how to produce your own video; or you can choose from a variety of currently available producers. The following is a sample of people available who want to help you.

1. Chris Steel, producer of metal and rock.

2. Gustavia Miller, producer of pop; projects completed include The Mayor's Ball, The Bite, and Sound Of Portland.

3. Carroll Gleason, producer of Christian music, regularly produces Rolling Thunder.

4. Todd Korgan, producer of jazz.

5. Brian Goal, producer of jazz, experienced in filming street dance.

KTZZ TV 22/Bombshelter Videos (206)623-4556. Frank Harlan wants your already produced videos on 3/4" format. Independent, college projects, and "MTV rejects" are encouraged. The airplay is FREE.

KUTF TV 32/Madison Street Theatre (503)364-1000 or (503)585-3232. Contact Sheryl Stewart at the former number, Janis Becker or Ted Watson at the latter number. They are seeking musicians performing all styles of Christian music, either live or on video. The airplay is FREE.

"Set a goal and stick to it. Stay out of sleasy situations. Don't follow a trend, start one! Seek your own originality. Keep in mind that if you do what you love, the money will follow." (Bobby Castaneda, KPDX TV, Portland, OR)

5. Make sure all cassettes, CD's, records, and reel to reels have your name, address, and phone number on the product. Also include the titles of the songs, their authors, your registering company, and release date.

If you are not ready to approach commercial radio, but do have a demo tape, contact college, public, and alternative radio stations in your area. Some have programs that feature local artists and are rather eclectic in nature; they do not demand the polished edges that commercial radio does. You may even be able to do interviews on these stations, which could lead to a concert (where you could sell your tapes). Music stores, schools, churches, and any clubs that you are involved with may be willing to post your concert itinerary.

RADIO EXAMPLES

The following are examples of area radio stations open to playing regional product and their criteria for airplay.

KMHD, Portland, OR. (503)661-8900. Tom Costello or Greg Gomez accept CDs and good vinyl of *jazz* music.

KBMS, Portland, OR. (503)222-1491. Ron Lee wants *funk and urban* on CD, vinyl, or cassette.

"To gain a local following, make sure your material is good, your sound appeals to the audience you want to reach, and that you offer something new or different from other bands." (Bobby Castaneda, KPDX TV, Portland, OR)

KINK, Portland, OR. (503)226-5080. Carl Widing is looking for CDs of *jazz-fusion* and *A/C album-*orientation.

KOAC, Corvallis, OR. (503)737-4311. Fred Child is looking for *anything* by Northwest musicians, from home-made tapes to studio-quality albums.

KBOO, Portland, OR. (503)231-8032. Rhonda Kennedy (a.k.a. Rhonda "X") accepts *anything* from Northwest musicians, any style, any format.

KCMS/KCIS, Seattle, WA. (206)546-7350. Lynette Morgan would like Northwest *christian* music for the Northwest Saturday Night program.

KKRZ, Portland, OR. (503)226-0100. Bill Kezley is looking for up-and-coming Northwest artists who have record contracts and play *pop, CHR,* and *rock.* Product must be on CD.

KUIK, Hillsboro, OR. (503)640-1360. Lisa Dupre accepts vinyl, cassette, and CD's of *A/C* musicians who have a great local following.

KCCS, Salem, OR. (503)365-1000. Sheryl Stewart is looking for *christian A/C, MOR,* and *CHR* music with strong lyrics, on CD or vinyl.

"Today's successful bands are professional, though not necessarily slick. They have a natural showmanship and a positive attitude. Some acts are dead in the water because they do not have that honest, genuine feel about them." (Fiona Martin, *Willamette Week,* Portland, OR)

KUGS, Bellingham, WA. R&B, folk, jazz, fusion, blues, blue-grass.

KGHP, Gig Harbor, WA. jazz, adult alternative.

KNUA, Seattle, WA. contemporary instrumental jazz.

Call the radio stations, video and television programs and publications before you send any materials (see booking chapter for phone technique). These businesses often undergo format changes, personnel changes, etc., and it would be in your best interest to address your correspondence to the correct person and to the right music format.

Some terms you may need to know include: A/C "adult contemporary"; CHR, "contemporary hit radio"; R&B, "rhythm and blues"; AOR, "album-oriented rock"; MOR, "midde-of-the-road".

"It's not such a bad thing to be 'just a local talent.' There is a place for people that have an impact in their local community. You're not a failure if you don't have a world-wide audience; in fact, that much pressure puts a lot of strain on artists. Don't be 'just passing through'...enjoy where you're at and play for whoever will hear you." (John Smeby, Reality Rock Program, Redlands, CA)

So, how long have you been performing 'Noise'?

WORKSHEET

1. List local and regional music publications.

2. List local and regional daily newspapers.

3. List local and regional weekly newspapers.

4. List local and regional college newspapers.

5. List national music publications of interest to you.

6. List cable access and television programs that currently have local and regional music shows. List stations that are open to the idea of carrying such programming in the future.

7. List local and regional commercial radio stations that play your style of music.

8. List local and regional college, non-commercial, and public radio stations.

(You may need to use a separate sheet of paper for this exercise.)

Recording

When should you consider recording your music? How much will it cost? What is the best, least expensive, most widely accepted format these days? How should you go about choosing a studio that is right for your music style and needs? These are a few of the questions you may be asking yourself now or possibly will ask yourself in the future concerning recording.

Your Recording Goals. The biggest problems for first time "Recorders" are lack of money, lack of goals, and/or lack of planning. Before you consider doing a recording ask yourself:

1. Why do I want to record? What goal will I reach by recording my music?

2. How am I going to pay for the recording?

3. Do I want to do a scratch demo, or do I want to do an all-out album project?

"It takes about 10 years from the point you decide to make music a career to the point you actually have a chance at national exposure. Bob Dylan started in music in 1964, and never really sold many records until 1973. It takes about 5 to 10 years AFTER you get a record deal for you to really get the familiarity you need to make it national. As a record company, we are looking for "lifers," not a short-term act who want to make it big and then retire." (Mike Demonico, Milk & Honey Records, Franklin, TN)

4.   Am I practiced and ready for the possibly grueling hours in the studio?

5. Do I have a marketing/sales plan to move the 5,000 albums to the consumer, so they don't end up collecting dust in the attic?

6. Do I have a commitment from my band and support system so I can tour, and in so doing, play my music and sell my albums? Or do I have enough local work available that the music basically sells itself?

Financing Your Recording.

The following are ideas for financing your recording.

1. If you are the musical spokesperson for your association, church, or community group, they may help foot the bill for your album, so they can spread their message through your music.

2.   Borrowing from your own savings and paying yourself back monthly with interest is a great way to invest in yourself, plus make a profit!

3.   Some studios are open to working with you using payment schedules, special plans, or the use of credit.

4. You may consider working with some of your musical friends to cut a "sampler" album, and split the cost between you. (You could record a "Portland Rock Album", "Portland Jazz Album", "Portland Wedding Album", "Portland Classical Album", "Portland Rap Album", "Portland Alternative Ethnic Whale Music Album"....) Then send the album project to appropriate radio stations, national and local trade magazines, retail, and sell them at each of your concerts. This could even be a special fundraiser project for well-established bands.

5. A Christmas sampler album would be a good bet to reach a wide variety of radio stations and consumer homes.

6. Sell your albums in advance, and use the money to help record the album. Pass out order cards at your concerts that offer your upcoming album at a reduced price. Interested buyers pay then for an album which is mailed to them in the near future. This method will also give you a list of future buyers, and start or add to your current mailing list.

The Cheapest Demo

Many times semi-professional musicians have four and/or eight track recording facilities in their homes and would be available to engineer inexpensive demo's.

Do keep in mind that your demo will probably not sound like the stuff you hear on the radio...it will be a scratch demo. If you want to have a slick sound, you need to consult a professional recording studio.

Copyrighting Your Songs.

Sometimes copyright forms are available at your local recording studio or from the library. They are free. You can also order forms by writing: Register Of Copyrights, Copyright Office, Library Of Congress, Washington, D.C. 20559. You may want to call the Copyright Office and leave a message that you would like a **Music Copyright form** sent to your address (202-707-9100). To have the forms processed costs around $10.

Registering Your Songs.

All songs played on the radio must be registered so that the authors can recieve royalties.   Performing Rights Organizations include:

ASCAP: 1 Lincoln Plaza, New York, NY 10023, *or* 2 Music Square West, Nashville, TN 37203. ASCAP has a membership fee and an annual fee.

BMI: 40 W 57th Street, New York, NY 10019, *or* 10 Music Square West, Nashville, TN 37203. BMI has a $25 life-time membership. You must think up an original registration name and register each song you write under it.

SESAC: 11 Music Circle So. Nashville, TN 37203.

"It's cheaper to record here than in New York or Los Angeles. I think the future and economy of Portland will be enhanced as the local music scene continues to grow." (Kathy Traylor, Moe's Pianos, Portland, OR)

Professional Recording Studios

Consult the phone book under "Recording Studios", and ask others in your music associations for referrals to studios.

Check out local and national music publications for articles on studios, and advertisements. Each studio has its own unique sound and philosophy, and it is good to interview several studios to make sure the goals, music styles, and lifestyles match up. You will basically be living with these guys for awhile, so make sure you can get along with them. To give you an idea of studio styles in the Portland area, the following studios were interviewed.

Spectrum Studios, **Mike Moore**   (503)248-0248.

Mike Moore has an ear for music. He grew up in the Bay area and enjoyed "local" artists like The Grateful Dead, Quicksilver, and Jefferson Airplane. Mike moved to the Portland area because he likes the pace and sees potential for good business here. The following are excerpts from our conversation.

On The Business: "Take a realistic look at yourself and the music business. It's tougher than it's ever been. If you aren't really innovative and really good, you'll never make it. Some people have big bucks and that's how they make records and get airplay, but they are just a few. You've got to know what your goals are and have realistic, not naive, ideas and attitudes. This is not a friendly business at all; it's cut-throat."

On Attitude: "Doing an album is like being in a relationship, and the kinder everyone is the better the album goes."

On Music Taste: "I see the music industry shifting back to the 60's Folk-Blues gut-level sound. I personally enjoy and collect everything from jazz to rock to country if it is an incredible recording. I also collect records that have gone platinum."

On Books To Read: "The best books on the subject I know of are *This Business Of Music,* and *The Platinum Rainbow.* You can get both at Powells' books. Also, PCC Cascade Campus has a great class on recording."

On Goals: "I want to attract business from Los Angeles and New York to the Northwest. That's where the money is. Whether it be music or film, they have tremendous budgets to work with, and we have the local talent to do the job."

Northstar Studios, Scott James-Hybl (503) 760-7777.

Scott James-Hybl is originally from the Bay Area and came to Portland with his family to attend Western Conservative Baptist Seminary. While here he worked with Jeff Johnson to build Ark Records in Tigard. Scott started Northstar on his own to fullful his dream of doing larger and varied projects. Scott is known internationally for his digital sound samples, and such artists as Chaka Kahn and Miles Davis have used his services.

On Simplicity: "I'm open to doing sampler albums and working with musicians' budgets. Northstar even has something as simple as professionally recording your voice with an accompaniment tape/trax!"

On Recording: "No matter how good the drummer or how fancy the equipment, it will be a waste of money to do an album with a bad producer or engineer. Listen to several studios, and a completed album project before you agree to have them do your album."

On National Advertising: "National advertising is actually a networking tool as opposed to a money-making tool. It makes people within the industry aware of your presence, but unless you're touring nationally, it doesn't guarantee that your product will be widely accepted nationally by retail."

On Money Made: "Very few groups are able to make money and survive. The light and sound technicians are the people making the money at a concert. Know your goals. Financially, to start out you can do just as well, if not better, regionally rather than nationally. An example of concert income would be: one concert per week for a year, $100 per concert equals $4,800 yearly. Net income of your first run of tapes would be about $7,500. Net income of your second run of tapes would be about $13,000. In one year your income would be $25,000. Make sure you plan for your second run of albums because it makes a big difference in your income."

Recording Examples: "We had one group spend $1,000 on an album, taking one weekend to complete it. They had good graphics, packaging, and sound. They sold out of that album, and came in to record two more albums, spending $7,000 total. They made a return of about $90,000 by selling cassettes at their concerts. We had another group that spent about $15,000 on one album, but had poor packaging and graphics. They did not sell as well at all."

Sound Impressions, **Dan Decker**   (503) 659-5953.

Dan Decker and his staff believe that a musician should be prepared before entering the recording studio. Sound Impressions provides FREE pre-production meetings and a guide with helpful hints on the recording process.

On Estimating Studio Cost: "It's hard to estimate studio cost...it depends on a lot of factors.   Do you want only piano and vocals?   That's really easy and goes fast. However, if you want to do 25 takes per track, bring in a horn or string section, the expense will add up. Also factor in set up time, defining and equalizing sounds, the number of tracks, instruments, complexity of production, and mixdown time. Don't believe that you can do it in two takes; even the best studio musicians take several. Also don't scrimp on the time needed per song."

On Album Size: "Three or four songs that sound killer are much better than ten songs that were rushed."

On Clients Who Record At Sound Impressions: "We record for such locals as Dan Balmer, Van Walraven, and Johnny And The Distractions. We're working on many other projects including Nero's Rome. We have clients from outside Oregon; we even have one that comes from Germany to record with us."

On Styles Of Music Recorded: "We do all types of music, solo to ensemble, metal to jazz."

On Taking Your Music Professionally: "In the music world, you are a product that a record company is going to risk investing their money in. Just like selling any other product, the record company wants to optimize the return and minimize their risk of loss. Most of the overnight 'Cinderella' stories have many years of hard, well-directed work behind them. If your musical goals are not being met, ask yourself why. Be your own best and most often-consulted critic. The industry is looking for serious people with a plan and discipline. A professional sounding demo shows you are organized and care about your music. Record and radio people have a lot of demo tapes to go through each day, and basically the best sounding tape wins."

"The door to musical success opens and closes so quickly. A 'hit' only lasts 12-17 weeks, and if you don't have a follow-up, or past successes, you are forgotten. Make sure you have a solid job to fall back on. Do what makes you happy and then do your music on top of that. Put your 'music' money into a retirement fund, or a college fund for your kids. Sometimes the pressure to make a living out of music is almost unbearable, and it takes some of the pleasure you originally felt away. I've found that the less a person is worried about making it in music, the better music they make." (Jerry Christy, Pinnacle Road Records writer/composer, Holtwood, PA)

Entertainment Attorneys

Many musicians consider entertainment attorneys as the quickest and most effective way to get their music exposed to the right people.

Look in the phone book, ask your friends, and consult recording studios for a reputable entertainment attorney in your area.

David Wray is a Portland entertainment attorney open to helping local musicians. He is included in *Who's Who In Entertainment,* and has contact with the Vice Presidents of all the major record labels and publishing companies. For a reasonable fee, he will listen to your music tape, critique it, and give you constructive feedback.

Since most national labels do not accept unsolicited material and only want to deal with serious musicians, an entertainment attorney may be the best way to go if you are aiming at "The big record deal".

"Music is an investment, and you must have money to invest in it. If you want to start a car lot, Cheverolet won't give you 50 cars to start with, you've got to buy them. Sometimes what musicians want is to spend a few bucks on a cheap tape, and then expect radio to give them thousands of dollars worth of free advertising. It just doesn't work that way." (Lew Davies, KPDQ Radio, Portland, OR)

Vinyl, Cassette, Or CD?

This subject is best summed up by Portland producer and recording engineer, Rob Farley.

"Don't use vinyl, it's an outdated format. Cassettes are O.K., but if you are semi-professional, I would strongly encourage the use of CD's. Another option is to use a limited pressing of CD's for promotional work and radio airplay, and cassettes for retail, since cassettes sell well at concerts and in stores due to the lower unit cost. You are doing well if you sell 15% of your concert attendance." (Rob Farley, Producer/Engineer, Portland, OR)

"Use your first tape as a barometer to see if you should continue recording. You may not break even on your first album, but if you have a viable product, your second album will probably do well. Then people will want to purchase your first album also." (Royce Mitchell, Musician, Portland, OR)

"Under contemporary standards, a song has a better chance of being put on a radio or video playlist if it's under four minutes long." (Ted Rogers, KPDQ Radio, Portland, OR)

"Don't go out and try to raise $40,000 for an album thinking, 'If only I had an album, then I'd have a ministry!' The ministry has got to come first. I know of people with attics full of this kind of thinking." (Laural Peters, Musician, Seattle, WA)

**They'll love me
yeah yeah yeah**

WORKSHEET

1. Why do you want to record? What goal(s) do you want to achieve?

2. How will you pay for the recording?

3. List local and regional recording studios. Investigate national recording studios that are well-known for your style of music.

4. List in order of importance qualities you seek from your recording experience. (i.e. staff open to new music ideas, studio available for all-night sessions, moderate price, engineers with good attitudes...)

5. List entertainment attorneys in your area.

Musicians

Sometimes the best way to understand what a local musician goes through is to talk to a local musician. Musician support groups, clubs, and associations bring together all kinds of fun, creative people. (See chapter on support systems)

The following Northwest musicians offer their experience, comments, and encouragement.

BRIAN DAVID WILLIS

Brian David Willis is a vocation-oriented musician, a professional who performs rock music. His goal as a producer is to work with bands that have contracts with labels that have budgets, so he can afford to go all out in his creativity. His goal as a musician is to be true to his talent and to encircle himself with centered, peaceful people.

Some of Brian's earliest memories were that of his sister and mom playing the piano. Brian used to plink around at the keys and tap rhythms on the cabinet, so his mom started him on piano lessons also. When his folks could not afford lessons, his older brother paid for them. The family was supportive of his musical talents - and then he began playing drums. His mom saw potential with his slick sense of rhythm and that he actually would practice. His drum teacher was a main influence on Brian's musical life and would take Brian to clubs as the drum player (the teacher would play guitar). Brian dabbled in trumpet, trombone, guitar, bass, and sax, but always came back to his first love...the drums.

Brian's band experience started in grade school. His class had a sock hop, and his "band" played 3 or 4 songs. Then they played a few records, and the band played the same 3 or 4 songs again. His first paying performance was when he was thirteen and played at a teen dance club.

Brian's musical influences were primarily from the Beatles and the Beach Boys because he enjoyed their energy.

His adult musical life has been quite exciting: a national hit with the band "Quarterflash", and his current band "Caryl Mack" has kept him busy beyond his regular tasks of record producer, husband, daddy, and "Musician Boot Camp" coordinator.

Comments From Brian:

What Makes A Good Concert: "When Quarterflash was opening for Rick Springfield locally at the coliseum, the crowd went nuts; we could hardly hear ourselves over the screaming! It felt good to have the local support, and we were rather stunned by the welcome. Also, at Madison Square Gardens we opened for Elton John. There's a certain aura about playing 'The Garden,' and I felt like I'd accomplished what I had set out to do."

On Attitude: "You meet the same people going up the ladder of success as you do going down - so be nice to everyone."

On Success: "Success in jazz is just as much respect as it is money; success in rock is if you're rich and 'the flavor of the week.'"

What Makes A Concert Bad: "At Baton Rouge, Louisianna, on Labor Day weekend, we did an outdoor festival. The weather was bad, and the attendance was worse; there were more portable toilets then there were people. We started playing before our sound was all hooked up and tested, so the sound was atrocious. Then we didn't get half our pay because the promoter lost so much money that he skipped town!"

On Spirituality And Faith: "When you're trying to get ahead, make a living, and embrace commercial aspects of trying to sell your art, faith and trust sometimes are the only things that can get you through. It's not easy to make a living. You hustle and work a lot of hours, you have to keep getting up after being knocked down, and you have to try to make money for your family. Sometimes things get bleak and you need to rely on faith. Keep doing your music as long as it's *right* in your heart. Faith and trust in God enables me to say, 'O.K., tomorrow I'll do this again, even though today was rotten.' If I didn't have faith, I would have chosen a more conventional and less hectic job by now...but music burns inside me like a candle that won't go out."

On Pitfalls: "Watch out for alcohol and drugs. People in ALL music face the same demons. You need to keep yourself in the best shape physically and emotionally if you want to really excel in music. You need to keep a clear head. A performer puts in more hours than most folks. At the end of the glamorous day, you go home and do all the normal things like deal with the plumbing, nightmares, and the dog's fleas. What looks so easy is actually a lot of hard work, or the result of a lot of hard work."

On Ego: "When things are good, don't take your own press seriously - nobody is that good. Don't base your happiness on your chart position, just pay attention to what you are doing musically. Don't try to respond to the latest trend or fashion because by the time you write it, record it, and distribute it, 'IT' is no longer in fashion."

On Songwriting: "As a songwriter your first 100 songs may not be that good. Keep practicing. Spend time churning out product and getting feedback just to learn about the process. Hear what you do well and what isn't so good before you try to make it big."

On Reading Material: "I read *Mix Magazine* and *Home And Studio Recording*. I find that a lot of the other magazines are more fluff than stuff."

On Booking And Contracts: "Ninetynine percent of the time it's word of mouth that gets me jobs, either studio referrals, friends, or people that have heard my work."

On Discouragement: "Allow discouragement to fuel your fire and passion for your art. Your family and friends may try to drag you down by saying that you are being foolish to choose a music career. On days you need a little extra 'juice', use their negative attitude to get you mad and then use the energy generated to go for your goals."

BONNIE KNOPF

Bonnie Knopf is a worship and outreach-oriented musician, a semi-professional who performs middle-of-the road (MOR) music. Her goals are to: Give glory to God, become an even better music communicator, and possibly see her music obtain national exposure.

Music is a part of Bonnie, "I ate, breathed, and wrote music." She could express her feelings and emotions, no matter how elated or depressed, through music. She took piano lessons beginning in the third grade, and at Centennial High School sang in the "C-Notes." At Portland State she sang with "The Norman Leyden Pop Singers," as well as singing at weddings, funerals, and Rotary clubs.

Bonnie feels that musically she was the most influenced by her high school music teacher, Dick Muhle. He told her, "You have potential," and those three words helped her to believe in herself. Bonnie was a go-getter in high school on the outside (involved on the dance team, homecoming and Christmas queen), keeping very busy so that she wouldn't feel the loneliness inside.

In college she came face to face with her own inability to make life "work" and decided to either end it or change it. It was then she decided to seek God.

Bonnie first discovered her music focus when she had some friends over and they asked her to play some songs she'd written. After finishing a song about moms that don't have time for their kids, she saw tears streaming down the face of her social-worker friend. The friend commented that she'd never been touched like that during a song, and that she sees the results of neglect every day at her job. Bonnie realized then that she could communicate to others what she held dear; that she could use music to teach, edify, and touch the hearts of others.

Bonnie was further infuenced spiritually by her husband's mother, Eileen Knopf, and a family friend, Ruth Calkin.

Bonnie now combines the music she loves with the purpose and meaning she's found, to form music full of forgiveness, love, and personal growth.

Bonnie has been involved in church music ministry for 14 years; leading in Sunday school music, praise and worship, and even training others to lead in worship. She has written choruses and seen them used in area churches.

Bonnie continues to take voice and keyboard lessons from Sue McBerry and Rob Farley. She feels it is important to continue expanding her musical horizons.

Comments from Bonnie:

On Recording: "I have a 4-track recorder, mike, and reverb unit which I use to compile my scratch demo's and compose songs. I've done the actual albums at Northstar Studios, with producers Dean Baskerville and Rob Farley. When you want to do a professional recording, my advice would be spend the money it takes to make a product worth listening to. Do it right the first time - it's much more expensive to go back and re-do it."

What Makes A Good Concert: "On a recent concert I really connected with the audience - it was US watching God work - a really moving experience. A good concert is when peoples' hearts are open and the music is meeting their needs."

Strangest Experience: "At a concert the sound engineer accidentally crossed some wires and whenever I hit a certain note the sound system would cut out. Finally I stopped the track and just pulled together some improvisation. I thought it was a disaster, but it turned out the group really liked it!"

What Makes A Concert Bad: "I hate it when there is a wall up before I even start to sing. When a church has a political undercurrent, backbiting, or spiritual emptiness, I just want to run and hide."

On Pre-Concert Prep: "I think through and pray before each concert concerning what God would want me to share. People don't come just for wind and words, they want words that count, and I want to communicate something worth their time."

On Attitudes: "Sometimes in musician circles there is a one-up-manship attitude of, 'I'm better than you.' I just die in those kinds of circumstances because I believe music is a gift, and we all have different ways of expressing that gift. Be open to growth with your mind and your heart. Ask your support system for their opinions; if they consider a lyric questionable, consider changing it. Don't be a know-it-all."

On Booking And Contracts: "I've never actually booked a concert. All of my concerts have been by request or personal invitation. I will probably have someone do that for me in the future."

JOHN DOAN

John Doan is a vocation-oriented composer and harp guitarist, a professional who performs new age instrumental music. His goal is to help his audience learn through his artistry to appreciate music as a participatory (as opposed to passive) experience.

ohn Doan's love for music and heart for people surfaced in his own back yard. As a child, the neighbor kids would form bands and play surf and rock music for each other.

The kids would go to "Betty's Music Store" and dream about what instruments and equipment they would one day buy. Betty generously allowed the kids to experiment with any equipment they wanted to try, and so "Betty's" became rather the neighborhood hang out. When all of Betty's music teachers left for the summer, she asked 16-year-old John if he would like to teach guitar. When he accepted the teaching job, he was immediately given nearly 30 students!

John went on to graduate with a Master's degree in music, while continuing to teach and perform. He has collected, researched, and performed on several dozen historical instruments, his main interest being the harp guitar.

John is a national recording and performing artist on the Narada label. He also teaches part time on the music faculty at Willamette University in Salem, speaks at schools, does music seminars, and once a year performs a Christmas concert tour.

Comments From John:

Most Asked Question: "From musicians, I get asked, 'How do I get a record deal?' I tell them it depends on their music style, goals, who they want to reach, and who they already know. You have to do your homework, and learn how to reach the correct people. If your music is different from the crowd, you have a better chance of being recognized and singled out. If you are doing something already happening, you won't be noticed as

much. Take your uniqueness and develop that. We are all made special and for a purpose. Don't imitate others' gifts; seek your own. Identify some aspect of yourself; you'll be the strongest in that particular skill because only you are made that way."

On Booking: "I have an agent in San Francisco who books my concerts, so anything I schedule myself is extra. I do a lot of self-booking for seminars, festivals, arts associations, schools, and workshops. I get referrals from others in the music business, from those hearing my album (albums are great calling cards), and through my education resources. One of the best booking sources is "The Booking Conference" sponsored by the Oregon Arts Commission (in Salem call 378-3625), which is a treasure trove of information and networking for the serious artist."

Recommended Publications: "I subscribe to *Dirty Linen* which has artist interviews, record reviews, and valuable information about where and when artists are playing." (For subscription information, call 301-296-6934)

On Pitfalls: "You work very hard to get work, and after you work, you're out of work."

Best Concert Experiences: "A radio station program director in Florida fell in love with my music and wanted to bring me in for a concert. However, the community was accustomed to rock and country, and so the station was taking a real risk on my Instrumental music, but they went for it anyway. Turned out they had a HUGE crowd! The audience really loved it, they had never experienced music like mine before. It was a big success for the radio station, the city, the program director, and me. Another great story is in the town of Drain, Oregon. A wealthy man donated money for a community center, and I was the debut act. Four

hundred people live in Drain, and tickets were sold by the local barber who would lather up his patrons while playing a tape of my music and telling them about me. When the barber got to the place of putting the razor to the gentleman's neck, he'd ask how many tickets the customer wanted to buy. Needless to say, we had most of the town at the concert, and the audience was very receptive to a type of music they had never experienced before. It was a very rewarding experience for me."

DEIRDRA DOAN

John Doan's wife, Deirdra, had many helpful comments about music also. Deirdra is John's number one fan, motivator, and marketer.

On Marketing: "Making your music and marketing it takes a little detective work. Maybe the reason people aren't coming to your concerts is because of something as trivial as lack of parking. It's up to you to research and keep your eyes and ears open to input. About the only way to get a major label's attention is through an entertainment attorney, an agent, or an artist who is already on the label. This is why networking is so important. Don't be an island. Learn from the mistakes and experiences of those who have gone before you."

Recommended Publications And Books:

"Kenny Rogers', *Making It With Music*;

George Martin's, *Making Music*;

Arnold Mitchell's, *The Nine American Lifestyles*;

Paul Hawkins', *Growing A Business*.

Also, once a year Willamette University has an entrepreneur's workshop which is very helpful, and I second the recommendation to contact the Oregon Arts Commission."

CARYL MACK

Caryl Mack is a vocation-oriented musician, a semi-professional who performs rock music. The Caryl Mack Band goals (Caryl Mack includes Caryl's husband Scott Parker and other band members) are to enjoy making music and to be the best songwriters, singers, and musicians that they can be, and to get a national recording contract.

Caryl Mack (the person) enjoyed a musical-family-upbringing of mostly a cappella music and singing harmonies with her three older sisters. Caryl Mack started piano lessons at four, entered lots of talent shows, acted in school plays, and just generally was involved in creating music. In eighth grade, Caryl and

her best friend played and sang in a talent show that led to work at small banquets and parties. Her first "real job" was singing and playing guitar at a Mexican restaurant for $3 an hour plus tips. When the business didn't go so well, her payment went to free food plus tips, and in a few more months the place went under. So she sang at a pizza parlor and played lots of Ronstadt, Carla Bonoff, and Carole King.

Caryl Mack and her husband Scott Parker traveled world-wide doing USO shows while in college. They traveled twice to the Pacific and once to the Mediterranean and agree that it was a great way to see the world.

Caryl, Scott, and guitartist Ronn Chick have been playing locally for over three years, and recently signed a multi-year songwriting co-publishing contract with Warner/Chappell music, so part of their goals are being realized even as we speak. Lee Schneider (bass), Brian David Willis (drums), and Joe Mower (keys), complete the current lineup in the Caryl Mack Band. Albums are available in local music stores.

Comments From Caryl:

The Best Concert: "I think our first show at the Roxy in Los Angeles is one of the best - not because it was a great performance (even now I look back and think AUGH!) but because of the excitement and energy the band felt. It was scary and exciting and electric."

The Worst Concert: "It's a tie; at a Portland restaurant there was hardly anyone in the audience, and we had major volume complaints from the owner. To top that off, a crazy woman ran up to the stage, toppling tables trying to get to our bass player, Todd Jenson. It was a weird and very long night. Also, at a club in Lake Tahoe in our old Top-40 band, they showed ski movies on a screen behind us during our sets! Plus we had major volume complaints from the club owner, a tiny stage, and no snow on the slopes."

On Band Goals: "We started out seeking the elusive record deal, and along the way we began to realize the amount of stamina and determination that it takes to just stay alive in this business. Our focus has changed these days; not so much to get a deal and become famous, but instead to enjoy making music and be the best songwriters, singers, and musicians that we can be. You have to just enjoy the process and not let that 'deal' be a carrot to you. It can't be the most important thing in your life. It's still a goal, just not an obsession."

On Music Style: "Be true to yourself musically. Strive to be the best you can be at whatever talent God has given you. Realize that in the big picture there are only a few who make the big bucks. Don't let big money be your incentive. Do it because you love it."

On The Music Business: "Meet all the people you can in the music circles and LEARN THE BUSINESS SIDE. You can't survive without knowing what's going on. Be hungry for constructive criticism, and don't be afraid to make changes as long as you remain true. Be objective and be informed."

VERSUS

Versus is a vocation and outreach-oriented band, semi-professionals who perform rhythm-and-blues (R&B) rock music. Their goals as a band are to continue to communicate their message to their audience and to become self-supported by their music.

The guys in the band are from a variety of family backgrounds, the common thread being a love for music at a young age. Most of them either had piano lessons or were involved in grade school bands.

Versus had its roots in the band Change Of Heart. After three years, Change Of Heart disbanded so members could pursue college educations. Versus was formed by bass player Mike Conner and keyboard player Bob Barnes bacause they missed having a band. Owen Wright, keyboard player, re-joined the band after graduating from college. Tom Teutsch, electric guitar, auditioned for the band after seeing a poster advertisement in Eugene. Christian Crowe, the youngest and newest member (drums) saw the group in Eugene when they were Change Of Heart and again when they were Versus. Christian talked with Mike and Bob after the concert and said that if they ever needed a drummer to call him. A year later they did, and after a month trial period Christian became the regular drummer for Versus.

Jack Shumate, original lead singer for Versus, left the band to become the full time youth pastor at New Hope Community Church. Mike and Bob now share lead vocals.

The band's sound has developed as musical tastes have meshed; classical, jazz, R&B, and rock.

They all agree that being friends and supporting each other by listening and being patient is one of the secrets of the band's success. They also do double dut - Bob gives the band haircuts, Tom does light electrical work, Owen does PR, Mike writes many of the songs and Christian does set up and tear down.

Comments From Versus:

"You need a commitment to each other and to a common goal and love of music. Being in a band is almost like being in a marriage." (Tom)

"Ask your support people to help by using their skills. Maybe they can book or confirm concerts, run lights engineer, give practical or technical feedback, give emotional or financial support, or any number of practical things. Utilize your support systems." (Bob)

"When booking over the phone, get as much information as possible. Write down a list of things you need such as: Set up time, price, loading time, directions to venue, size of stage, etc. We have a guide list of everything you could possibly need to know." (Owen)

"Music can be as powerful an addiction as drugs. Don't be obsessive. Don't cut loved ones out of your life. Stay balanced." (Tom)

"Don't tear each other down. I recently saw a drummer in the studio trying to do his best, and his buddies were laughing and harrasing him. Be patient and encourage each other. If something bothers you about a band member, and it's not that big of a deal, just forget it. Let some of the little things slide." (Christian)

"Look for people with the same fire, vision, and excitement about music that you have. Commitment is a major part of being a successful band, and being able to be vulnerable around each other. Always look for the best in the other person. You have to grow together and be willing to be wrong." (Mike)

"Go and see bands that you like and talk with them after the concert. When you know the guys in the band, it's not so scary to audition." (Christian)

"Be yourself. One can't expect to minister through music or any other means unless he/she is 'real' and not trying to be some kind of an ideal character. Gain understanding of the business as soon as possible. Some things have to be learned by experience, but a lot may be learned by talking to others. Learn endurance early." (Owen)

"We can get caught up in the 'work of the Lord' and forget the Lord of the work." (Mike)

"Make sure you show interest in what your spouse does Even if you don't understand what your spouse does listen." (Bob)

"My worst experience was during a Change Of Heart concert in 1985 when I forgot the words to the ballads and a cappella songs. Then I started laughing and couldn't stop. To top that off, I knocked a small pipe off the pipe organ and it fell and broke an overhead projector. But they still asked us back!" (Mike)

"Before our debut act, someone had played with the keyboard and accidentally changed the pitch down five keys. We didn't get a sound check before hand, and it really sounded bad until we figured out what had happened. DOUBLE CHECK YOUR EQUIPMENT BEFORE YOU PLAY." (Versus)

"We were hired to do a wedding reception, and naively expected to play our original music. But then everyone wanted us to play 50's and 60's hits, waltzes, and 'Tie A Yellow Ribbon' type music. We had complaints that we were too loud, too soft, too slow, too fast. BE SURE TO CHECK OUT WHAT IS EXPECTED OF YOU WHEN YOU ACCEPT A JOB." (Versus)

JULIE MCCARL

Julie McCarl is an outreach and vocation-oriented musician, a semi-professional who performs jazz and most styles of MOR music. Her goal is to help encourage others through her music.

Music was a part of Julie's life for as long as she can remember. When her family would go places in the car, the six kids (Julie has five brothers) were not allowed to argue, so they would sing instead.

The family would also gather around Mom at the piano and sing, and Julie was active in her church and various camps with music.

Julie began performing professionally on a "fluke." She was babysitting at Timberline Lodge, and the kids wanted to play outside. The only way Julie could keep them content was to play her guitar and sing. Her music was overheard by the manager of the lodge, and she was invited to sing for the adults upstairs. Eighteen-year-old Julie learned the standards and developed her Jazz music taste at that time.

Julie has shared music at hospitals, rest homes, camps, clubs, resorts, and at weddings and funerals. She once played for her cousin, who was a resident at Emanuel hospital for a month. The kids from surrounding rooms gravitated towards the music, and hospital workers told Julie later that it was good for the other kids to get out and about, interacting with the healing tool of music.

As a single parent it has not been easy to make a living as a full-time musician, but Julie would do it all over again if she had the choice.

Music has been a healing force for Julie, and she enjoys sharing that joy with others.

Comments From Julie:

On Saying No: "It's O.K. to say 'no' to doing volunteer work. Everyone needs time to relax, and music, though it's fun, is just as much work as anything. Give yourself time to relax."

On Faith: "Faith is a very personal, strong thing for me. I believe one needs to own the dynamics of one's belief system, instead of doing what others say without a thought. Faith has brought me comfort, love, and trust."

On The Music Business: "One of the toughest things to do is to get distribution of your album. (Editors note: Julie has an album available at several local music stores) Also, the business is sometimes associated with drugs and demeaning to artists . Musicians' spirits tend to be gentle, and they need to develop a shield of sorts to protect themselves from some amount of overpowering."

Publications And Resources: "I subscribe to The *Whole Earth Review*, and appreciate their integrity. (To subscribe, call 415-332-1716) Another great resource is the fourth floor of the downtown library - that's the music floor - and I've seen some of my favorite local artists hanging out there, catching up on their reading, technique, and style of playing. Lots of music is available to listen to, to play, and it's just basically a great place to learn."

JIM FISCHER

Jim Fischer is a vocation-oriented musician, a semi-professional who performs easy-listening music. His goal is to do more film scores, especially Hollywood film scores, and to continue to produce music that stands the test of time.

Jim remembers lots of music in his home and church (Jim's dad is a Baptist minister). In fact, his first performance was in a church Christmas program playing a Sears' snare drum while the organist performed "The Little Drummer Boy." When Jim was in the ninth grade he played bass guitar in a band for school dances.

Musically Jim was influenced by the radio and Orval Goodwin, who ran a music store in Vancouver, Washington. Jim also studied with former Portland musician Jeff Lorber for two years. Jim currently plays piano at Alexander's in the Portland Hilton, does free lance engineering and production, and enjoys time with his family. He has a Christmas cassette single available and expects to do a full album soon.

Comments from Jim:

On Musicians' Options: "It seems like you either perform, teach, or work in a recording studio. To perform, you've got to take all of your musical influences and mold them into a repertoire that your intended audience can relate to. To work in a studio, you've either got to buy your own or else do whatever you can to hang out in that environment - book their studio time, clean their bathroom, or get invited to sessions by a friend."

On Pitfalls: "To really succeed, you've got to have your own songs."

On Breaking Into The Music Scene: "Versatility is the key word. Know your given instrument really well. Set reasonable short and long term goals. Beware of drugs and alcohol. If you're really good at what you do, eventually you'll find a niche that you fit into, and are able to produce what people need in your 'musical world,' whether it be performing, teaching, or other services. Get involved in a church and professional organizations such as the Oregon Media Production Association."

On Booking: "I have an agent who does booking for me occasionally. I also get referrals from aquaintances. Be sure to present yourself in a business-like fashion in look and presentation. Advertise in the phone book. When customers call, be on the ball with demo tapes, delivering bids, and other correspondence. A trick Andy Gilbert taught me is always get buyers to state what their music budget is first, and then you'll know where they're coming from as far as money goes."

On Recording: "I have a small home pre-production midi studio that includes a 4-track recorder. I would recommend Ron Stevens at Cozy Dog Studios in Vancouver, Washington; Falcon Studios; or Spectrum Studios for larger recording projects."

WORKSHEET

1.   What was your greatest musical success?   What did you learn from it?

2.   What was your biggest failure?   What did you learn from it?

3.   What local and regional bands do you look up to? What national and international bands?   Why?

4.   What musical questions and struggles do you have? What resources are available to answer your questions and help solve your problems?

5.   What can you do to help "younger" bands in your local and regional area?

Retail

So now you have an album or tape available. How are you going to sell it? We have already covered some of this in the Media chapter. Many times retail outlets like you to be performing regularly, have radio airplay, have good product packaging, and fit in with their current selections. They may have a special section for local or regional artists. Many will take your albums on a consignment basis. You may want to keep your retail outlets informed of your concert and media activity.

Retail open to local and regional product include the following:

Locals Only, Portland, OR. (503)223-7289. They accept *any* Northwest music, any format, and any style. They will also sell your T-shirts, posters, and the like. Consignment only.

Music Millenium, Portland, OR. (503)231-8926. They accept any Northwest artists, any format, and any style. After 1991 all product will need UPC codes. Consignment only.

"Sometimes local musicians have been beat up and ripped off, and we want to set a trend to be friendly and accessible for the local musician. That's our goal." (Don Bankhead, Locals Only, Portland, OR)

Artichoke Music,   Portland, OR. (503)232-8845. They carry lots of local music, especially folk, ethnic, and world music. Consignment only.

Christian Supply, Portland, OR. (503)256-4520. Christian musicians must be regularly performing, need some radio airplay, need good packaging. Cassette and CD sell best.

Rockport Records, Portland, OR. (503)224-0660. They carry local music in punk, alternative, rock and ethnic styles. Cassettes sell well. Consignment only.

Dightman's, Tacoma, WA. (206)475-0990.   Have branches in Puyallap and Lakewood. They carry local and Northwest Christian music on cassettes and CD's. Consignment only.

Stiles Of Relaxation, Portland, OR.   (503)281-6789. They carry local music in the easy listening, classical, new age, and other "relaxing" categories.

Emmanuel Gospel Supply, Vancouver, WA. (206)574-1333.   Christian musicians must be regularly performing, need some radio airplay, and need good packaging. Consignment only.

Second Avenue Records, Portland, OR. (503)222-3783. Accepts local and Northwest product, especially underground, alternative, new age, and metal. Consignment only.

Getting Stores To Stock Your Music

Go in person to each retail, music, and record store to promote your album and introduce yourself. Bring a bio, picture, and a tape/album. Be low key and to the point. An example of how to present yourself to a retail or music store could be:

"May I please speak with the music buyer? Hi, my name is _____. I'm doing concerts in town, and just finished a recording project. I would really appreciate any feedback on the album. May I call back in a week to see what you think?"

Leave one album/tape, a picture, and a band bio with the music buyer for them to critique. Call back in a week to see what they think of your music, and if they would be interested in buying your album or taking your album on consignment. If they are interested, send them albums along with another bio, picture, and your concert itinerary for the next few months. Include any posters, and a few business cards for good measure.

Call back periodically to see how the product is selling. Ask if there is anything you can do for the store to help the product sell better. Suggestions might be: an artist album party, posters for in-store use, or an interview with you on a local station sponsored by the store.

Leave business cards with the store's music manager, so if someone comes to the store looking for a band to play for weddings, parties, etc., the store can give out your card, and possibly sell your latest album so customers can hear what you sound like.

Continue to call back and to send your concert itinerary for as long as you want a relationship with the store. Your correspondence keeps your name fresh in the store's mind, and keeps the door open for you to sell your next album to the store.

Creative Retail

Where else would your music sell? If your target market is country music, try places where country listeners would congregate; country clothing shops, truck stops, and country home furnishings stores would be possibilities. If there are country organizations that use auctions as fundraisers, donate a few albums to their cause. You will get free exposure, help out community organizations, and possibly sell more albums.

Your community group or public radio station may have fund drives that give a bonus prize to patrons who donate X amount of money. Give a few albums to the association, group, or radio station - your music will be "talked up" as a special prize to patrons, garnering you more free advertising and publicity. (See marketing and publicity chapter.)

Be sure to have tapes/albums available to sell at your concerts. (Check with the venue owner or manager to make sure this is OK) Get a friend to help sell the albums because you will be busy talking with fans after the concert and will probably not have time to do sales, too.

"If people can't buy your music in stores, then there is really no need to play it on the radio." (Lew Davies, KPDQ Talk Show Host, Portland, OR)

Investigate the possibility of selling your albums and tapes at Bazaars, Street Fairs, Saturday Markets, and other short-term shops that feature handmade or locally-produced products.

Consider doing a creative commercial for your album during your set. Make it short and to the point. Music sells - so use music to <u>sell</u> your music. Your audience will enjoy your creativity, and this type of a commercial would most likely be accepted and enjoyed by your patrons, possibly having your commercial become an anticipated part of your concert or show.

If you are doing original wedding songs, record one side of the tape with your vocals, and the other side with just the accompaniment. Make these tapes available at bridal shows, churches, talent agencies, and anywhere else wedding musicians congregate. Wedding music is always in demand, so find your market and present your product in a creative way.

Some businesses, including some bridal shops, have books you can put your business card in. Classical and folk musicians can keep especially busy in the wedding market.

"Are you doing concerts locally? If no one knows your name, your product will not sell well in the stores. Your album needs to be commercial recording quality; even if it is only voice and guitar, it must be produced well."
(Kathie Duncan, Christian Supply Store, Portland, OR)

**Have fun running the musical race . . .
a race where all who run are winners!**

WORKSHEET

1. What music stores carry local and regional product?

2. What retail stores carry local and regional product?

3. What specialty stores might be open to carrying your style of music?

Index

The music you make today
your children will live tomorrow.

ORDER FORM

Postal Orders:
Hughes/Taylor, Barb Hughes, P.O. Box 12550, Portland, Oregon 97212. (503) 287-0412

Please send _____ copies of *Music Management Made Easy*. I am enclosing $12.95 for each copy ordered.

Shipping:
Book rate $1.75 for the first book and 75 cents for each additional book. (surface shipping may take three to five weeks.)

Payment:
Check or money order.

Bulk discounts available.

order now